As I write this it's Christmas Eve in Oklahoma and fixin' to snow…don't get much snow in Oklahoma.   When it does snow I'm immediately transported to New England. I am blessed to be closely related to both continents and treasure them both. I kind of think of myself as an Okiefied Yankee.

You may have read slightly different versions of some of these poems in earlier editions or read some of them in such magazines as *YANKEE, MAGICAL BLEND, QARRTSILUNI, THORNY LOCUST, OKLAHOMA TODAY, BYLINE* and *CALIFORNIA QUARTERLY.* Other poems you will read in this edition are brand new. May the Powerful Goodness bless them!!!

I have fun doing this poetry thing. One has to be whacky to write *good* contemporary poetry and quite whacky to write *great* contemporary poetry. I haven't accrued sufficient wisdom to wish myself quite whacky but am glad I don't have to worry anymore about what others think and am guaranteed, at least so far, a monthly Social Security check for booze, cigarettes and some occasional, albeit necessary, hors d'oeuvres. I shall render unto quite whacky due consideration at the right time if longevity allows..

Thanks to my lovely and sweet friend Jane Porter at Cartridge World™ for her support through the years. This is a non-commercial book but I feel I must tell you of the savings and quality merchandise available at Cartridge World™. You can cut your ink and toner costs by somewhere around 50%. Give them a try…you won't regret it and everything's guaranteed.

Also by Dick Brown

EATING THE LIGHT

SEA OF JAPAN

HOUSE OF SPARROWS

KENOSHA POEMS

THE OHIO OF THE MOON

BROKEN ARROW NOCTURNE

BREAKING AND ENTERING

NEW AND SELECTED POEMS

ELEVEN DOMESTIC POEMS

BECOMING INVISIBLE

WINTER POEMS-2004

THIS MINDS BLOOD

UNSOLICITED MANUSCRIPTS

SALAD MANIA

MORNING RUSH

WHAT KIND OF TREE IS HAPPENING TO ME

WITHERING MANOR

WITHERING MANOR

Grayhair Press
Broken Arrow, Oklahoma

Published in the United States by Grayhair Press. ®

Grayhair Press® and colophon are the property

of Grayhair Press. ®

Library of Congress Cataloging-in-Publication Data

Brown, Richard

Withering Manor / Dick Brown

ISBN 978-0-9843260-1-3

Printed in the United States of America

First printing

Ink Cartridges...Jane Porter @ Cartridge World.™

Cover photo...Lynn Ann Brown

Book design...Dixie Collette

WITHERING MANOR

CAT & TURKEY

This clanking Oklahoma bell
bobs atop a Tulsa sea buoy.
In the overall scheme of oceans
a nine something something.
Divicular finny bells dive
into maws of great gray gulls.
The bobbing rhymes with cat and eye
making one think a cat thinks by doing,
believing at times its invincibility.
Believing in the feline goddess Bastet,
defying tradition, tom, tit and cataract.
This black cat is scratching its way
along some patio taking on a sound
similar to that of turkeys gobbling.
Have you ever eaten cat meat?
Gobble-gobble, gobble-gobble-gobble-gobble.

TOSSUP

She was torn between going west
> for the Miss Obese U.S.A. pageant
> and picking up a pen to write lean.
She couldn't afford a cargo aircraft
> to get her to the Tulsa fat festival
> as she weighed over four seventy
> and it's iffy-per-lb. over these days.
> In her case, the lean was one ten.
> Since picking up the pen to mean
she's lost three hundred----is lean
> and currently working on a sonnet
> about Oklahoma and the real thing
> sweepin' down the plains to a creek
she's been up, paddle-less, seventy years.

MEOW

I've been staking out this poem
all morning. It's been playfully
biting me on the neck, lapping
me there with sandpaper tongue.
It jumps to the floor as black cat
and I realize I've been afforded
probable cause for a day or two.
  I don't have any substance…
just poems--let me do what I will.
It's that black cat I brought home
from work one day a few years ago.
It throws up hairballs semi-regularly.
  Sometimes it turns dark purple
bouncing off one wall, then another.

MUSE AT THE OLD AGE HOME

He spent significant time
before mirrors making up.
If he didn't like the metaphor,
he'd remove it with cold cream.
It was reapplying he really liked,
removing, over and over, tweaking.
taste and smell red Revlon, L'Oreal.
Lips side to side and puckering.
Gay when nobody else was around.
These days he's resigned himself
to being emphysematous and straight,
residing at an old folks home
under the ruse of poetry.

AUTOPSY OF GRANDMA'S BOYLE

I.

Its center was a maze of whorled steel
where crown gear drove the chroniclers of time--
charlatans with weight and geared wheel
who sought to measure lives with tick and chime.

II.

We traced the clicking to a niche,
where pendulum halted crown in equal swing
and found Dame Gravitation was the beech
who rendered tick and chime from coiled spring.

III.

It's not some miracle we see and hear
as hands rotate around the ashen place,
but contrivance to prevent what they most fear,
who seek to keep us marching at their pace.

THE OKLAHOMA CITY
VETERANS REHABILITATION
CENTER OF THE MIND

Is trying to teach the boy,

who was afraid at night,

spoiled mother's-boy

and fraidy bobcat,

that next time he fights

he must kill the opposition.

But before he totally machos,

the young woman who told

him she came from Barbados

and held his hand as he wept

on her repentance shoulder

at the veterans' rehab center

was a beautiful colony.

He can't recollect her name or picture her

but remembers how warm it felt

as they walked along her beach.

THE ECONOMICAL
DOUBLE-DEEP GRAVE
Part 1

9 a. m.

At five feet and digging

an unmarked burial offers

mandible and coffin handles,

bunches of unidentifiables

and Christian ad hominems.

9:10 a. m.

At six feet and digging

earth-worm ectoplasm

frolics with metaphysica

in tight black pullovers,

necrobiotic prostitutes

pander to musty derelicts.

9:14 a. m.

At eight feet and digging

Vincent W illem Van Gogh,

envious of the dark

swirling strata

removes an earlobe.

THE ECONOMICAL DOUBLE-DEEP GRAVE
Part two.

9:22 a. m.

At twelve feet the sexton

squares off the new grave

and inserts a concrete box.

Planks along the edges

are covered with plastic grass;

the Frigid lowering device

is placed and straps tightened;

safety chains attached.

9:50 a. m.

In ten minutes, at St. Patrick's,

mourners will cross themselves

as an acolyte swings a thurible

and a priest beckons the numen,

ignoring the chronic coughing

that is pissing off et Spiritus Sancti.

The glads and carnations arrive.

9:52 a. m.

The sexton decides on cremation.

ABOUT ECHO

She loves soft music,

earned a Masters Degree

at Alleycat You

in Felidae Zen.

Her prayer wheels

have bird trills

and fridgets.

She's never used

catnip

or tokeless cookies

for metaphor.

Echo's a state of mind.

Be listening.

¶

The Phoenix obituary editor
doesn't believe in using them
and as mine will be in that paper
I've chosen to compose it myself.
There will be one of them
for each of the grandchildren,
and one for each other family member.
Oh yes, one for Swifty, the goldfish
mom bought at Woolworths for 5 cents.
Swifty oughta be worth Swifty's own
and if I include a blurb about Swifty
jumping from the bowl to the floor
and how Swifty flopped until noticed
those four or five years
(except the last excursion)
it would make for a sizeable one.
Oh, and I will not have passed away
or gone to be with some savior.
Dick Brown…will have, officially,
kicked the God-damned bucket.

¶=*The pilcrow is the symbol for paragraph.*

BALL AT WITCH CITY

Our partners in black
in keeping with the trend
toward occultisizing America
have applied amitriptyline
to their wrists and earlobes.
They wear Blavatsky teeshirts.
They've become wildflowers
at the Salem Wiccan Ball,
root-dancing
along a shady lane
between perfume
and a Black Sabbath tune
about electric pollination.
If they fall, they won't get up.

DREAM MINER

Down we go into Mrs. Tully's gravesite
where she clutches a rosary and dream.
Down through root and funereal debris,
ten inches at a time, shovel by shovelful
down the mildewed, tree feeding throat.
Tully must have some dreams down there
locked tight between barely recognizable
rosary'd, long, death-curled fingernails.
Clavicle, ankle bone and root land,
casket handle, nylon stocking land.
Lady Tulley's skull has been separated
from its mandible, from its dental gold:
a moldering, light brown earthen carafe
full of dark, moist and secret compost.

ONE LINERS

COUPLETS

TERCETS

and

A HAIKU

or

TW O

Gossip is a socially transmitted disease.

Becoming elderly is hereditary.

Love is a difficult stain to remove.

Do you dare believe
you're wise enough?
You bet.

The poet, Dylan Thomas,

never wrote

of Welsh geraniums.

I've always taken
heavy drinking
lightly.

My name is Palindrome.

I am a racecar.

I go both ways.

When all else fails,

try pornography.

Two clouds linger

over Oklahoma

in the missionary position.

I can't help being ourselves
but we're working
toward consolidation.

Bigotry is an orally transmitted disease.

Go ask

the clergyman

and you'll always get

an answer.

Go ask

the Zen Buddhist

and you'll always get

a question.

I told nymphalidae
far too delicate for today's wind
to land in my hair.

Broken many times
secret promises I made
solely to myself.

If there is magic
change its name to poetry
make it official.

A blue butterfly
too delicate for the wind
loiters on a rose.

I love poetry
she wears silky underalls
and has great nipples.

Peace is that moment, past and future
where there are no wars, no industry, no greed;
just grandmas and babies.

Sometimes we take leave of conformity
and create something original.

Sandpipers skitter along…

nervous that they'll miss

the next wave.

We stick our heads

out the door

and there is nothing.

A kitten is nothing more
than an ad hominem
with a pretty face and fur.

Planned parenthood, disease and homosexuality all help manage the population problem.

Beyond my patio
Sky takes her morning walk
with Cloud on a leash.

A red wasp
sips dewdrops
from a tulip spathe.

Hatred

is a scaleable

fence.

Why do the TV censors

blur out

breasts and nipples?

It's six o'clock in the morning
and we're listening to
the Mockingbird Tabernacle Choir.

THE ARCHDIOCESE OF SEABROOK BEACH
for Heather Hughart

blessed o'whelk

o'tidal o'pool

o'winkle o'alter

o'seaweed credenza

o'bellbuoy o'hymnal

o'breakwater missal

o'pipering priests

o'fried clam o'wafer

archbishop o'beachpail

monsignor o'shovel

o'quahaug o'blesser

o' sand and o' sensor

o'seagull and spindrift

o'ripple and nipple

o'froth and o'hisser

o'salty sea feather

o'spindrift o'mary

oh for o'crise sake.

UPS DIVA
For Lisa

The UPS dliva

alight on

Hickoly Avenue.

It be felonious

if flitalily

not used

to desclibe.

United Pahcil

bloun flitillaly

fly flew

on lacey ling

deliva

baby lobbins

and flya clackas.

lost in spindrift

one morning from a dune
i saw it walking the beach
kicking dry seaweed

i yelled good morning
but it didn't stop
it kept walking and kicking

oh to be a dry starfish
or bluefish bone
entangled there

one morning i saw it
kicking dry seaweed
it's not a dream

it dissolves in the mind

CASTING LURES

It's a lonely old voyeur
with nowhere special to go.
It urinates in its tub,
swims there, a sexual trout.

You've heard of it before,
but now, know it better,
having seen it rise, splash,
shining like glass, steam
evaporating from its sides,
laughing, fin and flipper.

Patrolling below the surface,
watching you
cast your soul.

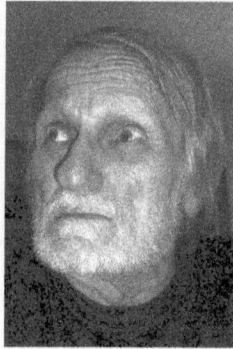

Lynn Brown photo

Born Richard Paul Collette at New Bedford, Massachusetts in 1941, Richard Brown attended schools in Andover, Massachusetts. After moving to Franklin, New Hampshire, Brown left high school in his junior year to join the Navy, serving from 1958 until 1962 as a boatswain and radioman. In 2009, Brown was awarded an honorary diploma from Andover High School. His affinity with alcohol and drugs would plague him for much of his adulthood.

Later in life during a period of sobriety achieved in AA, Brown would graduate summa cum laude from Connors State College at Warner, Oklahoma with a Degree in English. He would go on to attend Oklahoma University on a full regents scholarship but would be expelled for possession of a revolver in the final semester of his senior year. Richard Brown was named "Outstanding Creative Writing Student" by the staff at Connors State and upon request from the English Department at Oklahoma University, gave readings of his poetry at Gittinger Hall. Richard Brown currently resides at the Treetops old folk's home in Broken Arrow, Oklahoma.